Contents

Where the land meets the sea

Have you ever been to the seaside?
Did you see any of the creatures
that live there?   Where were they?
Did you know what they were?

Why do you think so many creatures
on the shore live inside shells?

LOCH DUICH PRIMARY

Under the Sea

Claire Llewellyn

SIMON & SCHUSTER

LONDON • SYDNEY • NEW YORK • TOKYO • SINGAPORE • TORONTO

Notes for parents and teachers
This book has a theme that threads its way through the subject of the book.
It does not aim to deal with the topic comprehensively; rather it aims to
provoke thought and discussion. Each page heading makes a simple
statement about the illustration which is then amplified and questioned by the
text. Material in this book is particularly relevant to the following sections
of the National Curriculum for England and Wales:

English: AT1 levels 1–2, AT2 levels 1–3
Science: AT1 levels 1–2, AT2 levels 1–3, AT3 level 3,
AT5 levels 1 and 3

In Scotland the proposals of the Scottish Education Department apply.

TAKE ONE has been researched and compiled by
Simon & Schuster Young Books. We are very
grateful for the support and guidance provided
by our advisory panel of professional
educationalists in the course of the production.

Advisory panel:
Colin Pidgeon, Headteacher
Wheatfields Junior School, St Albans
Deirdre Walker, Deputy headteacher
Wheatfields Junior School, St Albans
Judith Clarke, Headteacher
Grove Infants School, Harpenden

Series editor: Daphne Butler
Design: M&M Design Partnership
Photographs: ZEFA except page 15
Liz and Tony Bomford/ARDEA LONDON,
page 16 Konrad Wothe/Bruce Coleman
Limited, pages 24 and 26 Heather Angel
Line artwork: Raymond Turvey

First published in Great Britain in 1991
by Simon & Schuster Young Books

Simon & Schuster Young Books
Simon & Schuster Ltd
Wolsey House, Wolsey Road
Hemel Hempstead, Herts HP2 4SS

© 1991 Simon & Schuster Young Books

British Library Cataloguing in Publication Data
Llewellyn, Claire
  Under the sea.
  1. Oceans. Organisms
  I. Title II. Series
  574.92

ISBN 0–7500–0609–9

Printed and bound in Great Britain by
BPCC Hazell Books, Paulton and Aylesbury

7

Under the sea is dark

Each morning, with the daylight, we begin a new day.   There is so much to see and listen to.

Is there light under the sea?
How do divers see in very deep water?
What sounds might they hear?

Home to many living things

Many thousands of plants, fish and animals live in the sea. Some creatures are so small that you cannot even see them.

Which are the largest fish and animals in the sea?

Fish need to protect themselves

There are thousands of different kinds of fish in the sea – of every colour and size.

Fish prey on each other.
Can you think how fish might try to protect themselves?

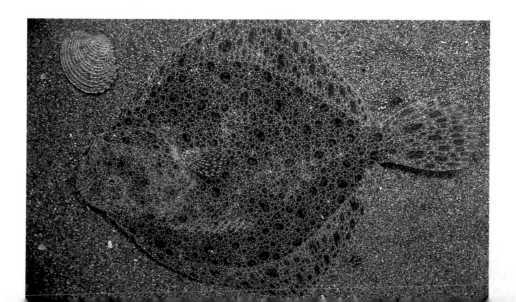

Streamlined for the sea

Have you ever tried to catch a fish
in a rockpool or pond?   Was it easy?
How does the shape of a fish's body
help it to move through water?

How do seals look when they move on
land?   How do they look in water?

15

Food for birds and animals

Many animals and birds who don't live in the sea depend on it for their food.

Have you ever seen birds dive into the sea for fish? How do they know where the fish are? Don't you wish you could dive like that?

Food for people

Every morning and evening, fishermen
all over the world set out to catch
fish, crabs and other sea foods.
It can be a hazardous job.

How many different ways of fishing
can you think of? Have you tried any
of them?

19

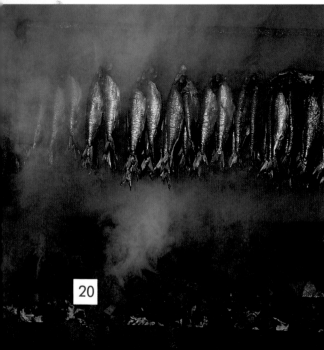

20

Buying and selling fish

Fishermen sell their catch at the market back at the port. The port may be a long way from the shops. What can they do to the fish to stop it going bad?

Do you eat fish in your house? Where do you buy it?

Fuel from the sea

It's not just food that we take from the sea.   Look at the picture of the oil rig.   Why has it been built in the middle of the sea?   Is there oil in the water?

Working on an oil rig can be dangerous.   Do you know why oil is so important to us?

23

Pollution of the sea

What does the sea look like when it
is polluted?   How does this happen?

What happens to the tiny creatures
of the sea when there is pollution?
What happens to the fish, and the
animals and birds which feed on them?

Breathing under the sea

Do you ever swim underwater? How
long can you hold your breath? How
does it feel? Some animals that live
in the sea can't breathe underwater
either. Do you know which ones?

How do divers breathe under the sea?

Stories from under the sea

People have sailed the sea for hundreds of years.   Sometimes their ships sank.   Can you think of some reasons why?

Divers try to find these shipwrecks down on the seabed.   Have you heard of any famous shipwrecks?   What can we learn from the wrecks?

Index